OUR SENSES

How Sight Works

Sally Morgan

PowerKiDS
press.
New York

Published in 2011 by The Rosen Publishing Group Inc.
29 East 21st Street, New York, NY 10010

Copyright © 2011 Wayland/
The Rosen Publishing Group, Inc.

First Edition

Editor: Nicola Edwards
Designer: Robert Walster
Picture researcher: Shelley Noronha
Series consultant: Kate Ruttle
Design concept: Paul Cherrill

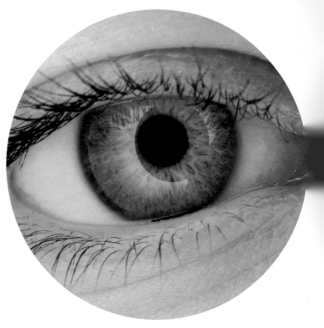

Library of Congress Cataloging-in-Publication Data

Morgan, Sally.
  How sight works / Sally Morgan. — 1st ed.
      p. cm. — (Our senses)
  Includes index.
  ISBN 978-1-61532-553-5 (library binding)
  ISBN 978-1-61532-559-7 (paperback)
  ISBN 978-1-61532-560-3 (6-pack)
  1. Vision—Juvenile literature. I. Title.
  QP475.7.M67 2011
  612.8'4—dc22
                                    2009044618

Photographs:
Cover: © Corbis; title page © David Gray/Reuters/Corbis; p2 Joey van Dun/istock; p4 Bananastock/Jupiter Media/ImagePick; p5 Denis Pepin/Shutterstock; p6 Joey van Dun/istock; p7 Ellen Martorelli/Getty Images; p8 (l) Johanna Goodyear/Shutterstock, (r) T-Design/Shutterstock; p9 Martyn f. Chillmaid; p10 © David Gray/Reuters/Corbis; p11 © Corbis; p12 Susanna Price © Dorling Kindersley; p13 Dmitry Pistrov/Shutterstock; p14 Matthew Luzitano/Shutterstock; p15 Vadim Koziovsky/Shutterstock; p16 Nick Hawkes/Ecoscene; p17 Darren Green/ Shutterstock; p18 photoaloja/Shutterstock; p19 Huib Theunissen/Shutterstock; p20 Martyn f Chillmaid; p21 altrendo images/Getty Images; p22 AFP/Getty Images; p23 Martyn f. Chillmaid

Manufactured in China
CPSIA Compliance Information: Batch #WAS0102PK: For Further Information contact Rosen Publishing, New York, New York at 1-800-237-9932

Web Sites

Due to the changing nature of Internet links, PowerKids Press has developed an online list of Web sites related to the subject of this book. This site is updated regularly. Please use this link to access this list:
http://www.powerkidslinks.com/os/sight

 Contents

👁 Seeing the World

We use our two eyes to see. Sight is one of our five senses. We use our senses to find out about our surroundings.

Our world is full of light and color.

As soon as you wake up in the morning, you open your eyes. What do you see when you look around?

Which fruits can you see in this picture?

Our five senses are sight, hearing, touch, smell, and taste.

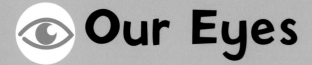 # Our Eyes

Look at your eyes in a mirror. Can you see the dark spot in the middle of each eye? This is called the pupil.

eyelid

eyelashes

pupil

iris

We blink about 12 times every minute to keep the surface of our eyes clean.

The colored part of the eye is called
the iris. Most people have irises that are
blue, gray, green, hazel, or brown.

What color are your irises?

How Do We See?

We need light to see. Light passes through the pupil to the back of the eye. There, a part of the eye called the retina detects the light. Then it sends a message to the brain.

Look at the difference in the size of the pupil in these two eyes.

n dim light, the pupil is large, so lots of light enters the eye. In bright light, the pupil is small to stop too much light entering.

In bright light, we protect our eyes by wearing sunglasses.

👁 Judging Distance

Close one eye. Try picking up an object in the middle of the floor. Now pick it up with both eyes open. Which was easier?

Judging distances is important in sports such as tennis and golf.

Our eyes work together so we can
judge how far away an object is.
This helps us to pick up objects,
play sports and perform tasks.

This boy is
using his eyes
to judge how
far he needs
to hit the
golf ball.

Seeing All Around

Put your arms out wide to your sides.
When you look straight ahead, you can see
your arms out of the corner of your eyes.

See if you can
see colored
cards placed at
the edge of
your vision.

Our eyes are
very good at
detecting movement
at the edge of
our vision.

We can see things in front of us, but nothing behind us. Many animals have eyes on the sides of their head so they can see in front and behind.

A horse's eyes are on the side of its head.

👁 Seeing in Color

People can see in color, but many animals see only in black and white and shades of gray. However, we can only see colors when there is plenty of light.

At night, in dim light, we cannot see colors.

People who are colorblind have difficulty seeing the difference between red and green colors.

A colorblind person cannot see the number 5 in this photograph.

More boys are colorblind than girls.

👁 Watch Out!

Bright colors, such as red and yellow, are easy to see. People use these colors in warning signs to alert us to danger.

This yellow sign warns people to keep away from electricity lines.

DANGER!
ELECTRIC
POWER LINES
OVERHEAD

Animals use warning colors, too. Many poisonous animals are brightly colored to warn other animals to stay away.

The bright-colored poison arrow frog is one of the deadliest animals in the world.

◉ Animal Eyes

Some animals, such as bears and rhinos, have poor eyesight. Others, such as owls and cheetahs, have very good eyesight. Many animals have eyes like our own, but some look very different.

Snails have eyes on the end of their tentacles.

nsect eyes are made up of lots of tiny
eyes that work together. These eyes
are good at detecting movement.

A fly's huge eyes give it excellent sight.

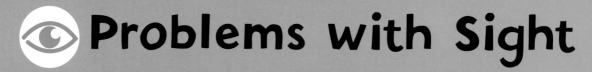

Problems with Sight

Many people do not have perfect sight. They have to wear glasses or contact lenses to see far away objects or to read.

Our eyes must be checked regularly to make sure we can see clearly.

Blind people are unable to see.
Some were born blind, but
others lose their sight through
sickness or in an accident.

Blind people use their other senses to find out about their surroundings.

Your Sense of Sight

Your eyes can play tricks on you. Look at these lines.
Which line looks longer?

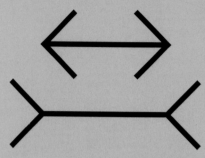

Now measure each horizontal line with a ruler.
What do you notice?

Look at this picture. Do the dots look as if they are moving?

Now choose one of the patterns and stare at the center of it.
What happens?

Find Your Blind Spot

Ask a friend to stand about 10 yards away from you. Cover one eye and walk very slowly toward them, looking at their face. Suddenly, their face will disappear.

This happens because you have a blind spot. There is a particular point at the back of the eye that cannot detect any light. When light lands on this point, you do not see anything. Normally, you do not notice this because you see through two eyes.

Glossary and Further Information

blind spot part of the eye where there are no light detectors

brain the control center of the body, found inside the head

colorblind unable to see certain colors

iris the colored part of the eye that surrounds the pupil

pupil a hole in the center of the eye that lets light pass through

retina the part of the eye that detects light

senses functions of the body through which we gather information about our surroundings

Books

Animals And Their Senses: Animal Sight
by Kirsten Hall
(Weekly Reader Early Learning Library, 2005)

The Sense of Sight
by Ellen Weiss
(Children's Press, 2009)

World of Wonder: Sight
by Annalise Bekkering
(Weigl Publishers, 2009)

Index